Salted Wakings

poems by

Judith A. Kennedy

Finishing Line Press
Georgetown, Kentucky

Salted Wakings

Copyright © 2019 by Judith Kennedy
ISBN 978-1-63534-892-7 First Edition
All rights reserved under International and Pan-American Copyright Conventions. No part of this book may be reproduced in any manner whatsoever without written permission from the publisher, except in the case of brief quotations embodied in critical articles and reviews.

Publisher: Leah Maines

Editor: Christen Kincaid

Cover Art: Nate Rayfield

Author Photo: Judith Kennedy

Cover Design: Leah Huete

Printed in the USA on acid-free paper.
Order online: www.finishinglinepress.com
         also available on amazon.com

Author inquiries and mail orders:
Finishing Line Press
P. O. Box 1626
Georgetown, Kentucky 40324
U. S. A.

Table of Contents

A Distance from the Waters 1

Freud's Dissenter 2

After Tsunami 3

Tribute to the First Woman of Auschwitz 4

Visitations on Waking 6

A Point is a Collapsed Infinity 7

What Is This *Therapeia*, This Attending To? 8

Final Summer 11

To See Only at the Termination of Things 13

Edward Hicks' Cemetery 14

Even This Turns to Something Else 16

The Chemist 17

Mathematics and the Girl 18

First Window 19

Council 20

The Priest Who Thought He Was Alone 21

One Circle of Flesh 22

Ancestor Walk 24

Augusts 25

This Sleep 26

In the Center of the Fire 27

Longfellow Pine 28

The Last Day 29

To the whisperings of the ancestors
never ceasing
so near

A Distance from the Waters
> For David Schoen who witnessed the floating
> light in Covington, Louisiana

Before the storm, it darts from trumpet vine
to bee balm, hovers with its wings
spinning like water wheels suspended
then drops and rises in perfect verticality.
Its tiny eye glances into human ones,
its phosphorescent green shines oneiric.

Survivors of Katrina crawl from under
homes split by ancient pines, from under
concrete that should have crushed
all of life. One man, at dusk, comes out
on the porch of his still-standing house
then rushes inside to awaken his sleeping
wife to witness:

> A wave of floating light that rises
> from beneath mangled trees,
> thousands of blinking fireflies,
> butterflies, a chorus of circling wings,
> triumphant hummingbirds.

Freud's Dissenter

In the nocturnal cathedral of dream,
a cast of characters climbs the rungs
of a ladder of darkness
where two worlds meet,
at an hour when the most austere
supplicate on rigid knee.

Like the monks of Nyssa
censured by Augustine,
he has no records of the great Councils,
he finds no place
in the houses of bishops, priests, or deacons,
except in sleep,
in solitary dream.

It is there he slips the wafer of light
into the mouth of memory,
eliciting communion
with the likes of Jacob,
sometimes waking
to a natural pillow of granite,
in the wilderness of modernity.

After Tsunami: A Salted World

If we would now step slowly
upon the skin
of this moving-through-the web-of-space-earth,
we would hear through our feet
the rumblings of every ground swell,
like the listening soles of the Inca, the Maori, the Hopi.

(There was a crashing undersea
and creatures knew and fled.)

It was a night with more than a single star,
with some constellation pulling forth waters.

What would the doctor Paracelsus say in such times?
What stars would he find floating in the red blood of life,
the celestial circulating through earth's veins
where one thought there was only the vacuity of matter?

And what would he say of all the hearted flesh
washed with salt and dissolved there?
Thousands returned to their origins in the sea:
the salt wash of tears flooding the earth
ten thousand times over
the Ten Thousand Things?

How will we ever rise again with such a weight of salt?
Or is this salted heaviness the element of soul,
sifting repeatedly,
merging with the shimmering moss of seas,
in this thickening and circulating universe?

Tribute to the First Woman of Auschwitz

It is a coincidence of numbers
that finds us together
on Lufthansa Flight 531,
as we scrape through cirrus clouds,
leaving the Viennese landscape,
crossing the tip of Greenland
toward the narrow line of Long Island.

After many hours of discussing
America and Europe, science and psychotherapy,
your disbelief in an afterlife, I begin to see
that your bird-like eyes are nestled
in folds of skin, folds that hold
in their recesses a history of gravity –
a history marked by the indelible ink
etched into your forearm,
and as these blue-black numbers
are reflected in my eyes,
you attempt to release what won't die
in the caverns of your memory;
and you begin to offer
the cutting shards of your story,
for which you must reach very carefully.

You say it was not your youth
that saved you, but that you were among the few
who found some mysterious inroad home each night,
back to the door of your Czech home
in the little town long vacated.
You say you would dream your way into village shops,
so that your back became numb to gun and stone,
so that on the long treks across fields of ice
your bleeding feet were wrapped in the warmth
of village visions.

And heroism? It is nothing but the other face
of Janus large with necessity.
But now you can return to your apartment in New York,
and every Wednesday meet with fellow survivors,
cook your own simple meal at night, go to the Met,
walk past Macys, go home and read another Michener novel.
Now you do not ask much of life;
you have seen it leap out at you – an actual Armageddon;
and you have seen it retreat, beaten back,
slumbering in generally good American times.
And you see the sleeping giant has a thousand eyes
in the sea of faces moving everyday along Fifth Avenue.

No, this indelible number, this immortal creature
can't be removed from you and placed in a D.C. museum.
It rides forever in the flesh of your invincible frailness.
And this number, which is now your skin,
appeals to the tiniest of children;
this boy who has wandered from his mother,
this child of Berlin, tugs at the soft, loose skin
of your grandmotherly arm.
You take both hands and cradle his yellow curls;
your fingers play in the ringlets there.
He slaps at your wrist and a light cascades
from your translucency and washes over him.
"No," you say, "I am bitter, but, I would never wish
upon my tormentors the five hundred deaths
that each one of us lived."
And as the plane touches down on the JFK runway,
you raise your hands and begin to applaud.

Visitations on Waking

She is hollow in the womb of sleep
as one hundred hummingbirds
waft about her ears, face, and fingers,
a whirr of buzzing and rising waves,
a melody that blues;
there is no voice,
no movement,
only the flitting of a tiny school of fish
in the tributaries of blood
that course her leaden flesh –
only the stirring of converging streams
pressing her flesh to move,
to break the dam of dream
into the river of waking light,
to shake loose the image
of silent children of white statuary,
seated on the rim of the fountain pool,
still, without breath,
crowned with mourning doves.

A Point Is a Collapsed Infinity

A point is a wavering place from which to glance,
an eye on a scale of E minor,
discrete on a line extending into horizontal time,
looping in allegro back on itself,
an image that penetrates its own mirror, and bounds back
across the Eastern sky, absorbed and unfurled.

It curls into this massive rock of roseate quartz
that weighs upon the mountain beneath power lines
during this crackling summer storm on the Potomac,
then rides north over the Hudson, near, yet distant
from the black, thrust up, Cambrian riverbed
hanging over the Susquehanna.

One point is many jettisoned from memory's watersheds:
it swims and quakes, leaps orbits,
moves sufficiently light in tents of dark transparency,
careens and rests winged in this golden piazza.

What Is This Therapeia, *This Attending To?*

How can I tell you
that your humanity
is not a disease,
that pain is not always
an indication of illness,
that your thoughts
are as they are,
turning one upon another
as they have been accustomed
to do, wearing darknesses,
and also opening their faces
to light?

How can I tell you
that your behaviors are not
bizarre as you run
from the dreams
that sift through the floorboards
of your childhood
into the time that is now?

How can I tell you
that you will only breathe
more freely with
love and care,
and that kindnesses
can be trusted,
and are not signs
of weakness,
that raging is not
power?

How can I tell you
that your laughter
is medicine,
that your welcoming me
into the travails of your
life is the beginning of
a journey that stretches not
according to Euclidean axioms,
but is a *circulatio* in the tower
of yourself, a stone staircase
that winds beside a lake,
and that sometimes the lake
turns up whitecaps
that slap against the tower walls,
but often the sounds are soothing
like amniotic waters.
How can I tell you
that we are all orphans
remembering
that enclosed safe space?

And how can I tell you
the greatest kings are found
in peasants' cloth,
that children are aged
and know exactly what
they need, and try in
whatever way they can
to get what they crave?
And how can I say
that we are all that child
and that king or queen in ragged robe?
And how can I restore the innocence
from your jadedness?
or rein the undisciplined horses
of your desires from dragging
you into the desert of loneliness?

How can I reveal to you what
I don't know myself,
or lead you to oases
that are hidden from my view?

Or, that often you are my guide,
that I go under the white caps
of my own struggles,
that I nonetheless swim
so closely with you,
and that we float on the
encrypted box of
Ishmael and Queequeg
and that the white whale
has already been slain
many times over?

Final Summer

The wet contours of your feet
caress the smooth floor of the kitchen
during your morning ritual,
a swim in clear water,
breakfast beneath the pines,
creating order after culinary chaos,
the tile tops glisten
like water at noon,
free of disturbance,
like your mind determined to glide,
stroke after amphibious stroke,
all space clear except
this window sill where you place
glass flasks, chips of quartz,
granite and sandstone
arranged around the violets
and begonias, the pencil holder,
and recipe box.

The night we go looking for you,
we find you near the hemlock
on your back,
with your eyes open,
staring at the deep sky,
Orion and the Pleiades.
Your mouth is a quiet smile,
your hands rest
over your heart
as if placed there
by some man of the cloth.
When you walk home with us,
there is a silence
that wraps itself around us
as a single cloak.

When we go to your lab
to collect your things,
we find our histories on shelves:
lamp shades and hair dryers,
refrigerator magnets,
girl scout compasses,
the salt and pepper shakers
you said one night
looked like Three Mile Island.
We bring your Geiger counter
and your wooden star finder
home to your desk
by the window.

To See Only at the Termination of Things

Twice now, as if from a great distance, I have seen
the uncanny, lemon-green grass brushed by black shadow
and dotted with the rapid flash of something like a child's white form
lifted high on a wooden swing suspended from old oak.
Twice, I have seen the variegated earth as if blood-filled,
pulsing just as my own breath was ceasing. And twice, with clay-like hands,
I have clasped another and have felt the room fill with a thickness
that can only be defined as a longing for what will be lost,
a sorrow for even the despised, a lament for non-existence.

This time, as we sit, I have been restored to equilibrium,
and you join the ranks of those selected by a dark hand.
You smile faintly and say that each moment of the day is like a thread
entwined with gold and lead for which you grasp not certain
of where it leads: only a chasm in the earth, if this,
or an entry into the vapor of extinguished things, or an arrival
at a mythic home about which you long ago ceased believing.
And as we kiss your brow, a softness washes over
the hardness of your features, and we tell you we'll return at two,
and you watch us go through the doorway to more living.
Now with your vision strangely fused with mine,
I take hold of the substance of things and watch the whiteness of sky
fill and cover the blue vacuity and raining sunlight,
and we find that just this sitting is enough, this breathing,
this inhalation of the extension of ourselves
into the parameters of other moving bodies:
bare trees, pores of earth, perhaps the Pleiades.

Edward Hicks' Cemetery
(Syracuse and Newtown Friends' Meetings)

I come home and find the biography of William Penn
wrapped in the same brown paper I sent it in,
with the words "deceased"
written across your name.

I had been neglectful, hadn't written or called,
and you had been busily working on the watercolor painting
you promised to be placed
in Newtown Friends Meeting.

They tell me you took it with you
to the hospice
and when you had finished with the final details
you dreamt this life away.

This evening I drive to the old Meetinghouse
of white and plastered stone,
near the cracking markers
of the Edward Hicks' cemetery.

It is late and the halls are dark and empty.
I decide to enter through the back doors
which open with the creaking of centuries-old
wood and hinges.

In this moment, I imagine you here,
arriving with your quick and spry- for-eighty step
as you tug at me to meet your aged
and weighty with wisdom friends.

I find the bench where you would sit
in silence, where you would rise
to speak, your voice quaking and ringing
with the gong of truth,

Now your presence surrounds like white lace
in the darkness where your words
and your life drop to the base
of a deep well of light.

Even This Turns to Something Else

You said many times how after yet another
tragedy in your life, you blame yourself,
think it is you, something about your very
presence causes people to die and perhaps best
to go yourself while driving the car near
the underpass on Locust Lane.
It would have been so easy you say,
but you thought of us
and held back the urge to die by the urge
to keep on loving the best you could.
The lush stretch of lawn was so green
out your kitchen window that first spring
and even the second and third thaws
and the full thrust of lilac and wisteria
were all about you as you held back from it
with a vacancy in your gaze casting
you far from us. And now in your
elder years, we sit under the apple tree,
the white azalea speaks for us,
a swallowtail finds your shoulder,
a hummingbird whirrs and stops
just at your eye level where it remains
for what seems to be a very long time.

The Chemist

Our father raises a glass of water to the sun
shortly after dawn when easier to observe

particulates swirl, rise as spectral globes
or drop as more or less solid, vanishing or

remaining, the chemistry of morning,
his curiosity peaking with silver clouds

crossing galaxies of liquid, universes
reversed with the telescope of the water glass,

each floating world the cause of scrutiny,
perplexities of hydrogen, mysteries of

oxygen far more comprehensible
than turns of fate or human love

Mathematics and the Girl

Her father stands at her bedroom door
with a slide rule, graph paper, and a box of pencil leads.
She sighs and looks down at her long fingers that wander
the roll top desk at night. The blue moons of her nails move
in the dark, wooden drawers finding torn slips of verse,
smooth sea stones, a hand painted card from China.
She takes the card and runs her fingers across its rough surface
feeling the thick, dried oils, imagining the touch
of the delicate brush. She prefers, she thinks, the brush
to the lead, the brittle lead necessary for correct, conclusive,
arithmetic results. Now she dips her finger into a pool
of spilled ink that runs into the spiraling contours
of her flesh, transgressing perfect angles and degrees and certainties.
Her father sighs. She thinks the lines of blue form a destiny
in the skin, reaching deep into the smallest of the small,
into the places that the digits of Euclid cannot sense,
like the lilac and light that wake her at her desk this April morning.

First Window

The window slides easily
into the aroma of
lilac trees and early
as the sun wakes upon
the white fence and praying
poplars as first light
slips through screen
across embroidered cotton
of her single bed.

The window slides like
whispers till there are none,
lets her climb down easily
into the wet grass
before black collie
and others inside stir,
before church bells,
before there is a chance
to remember the first
sliding of windows.

Council

You tell me with your eight-year-old voice
that you haven't played on this island
in two hundred years.
You say this with a certainty
that reaches beneath the ground
into the flow of this muddy river
that slides to the Chesapeake
along the same soil
that rested here untouched
before the Susquehannock.
And I begin to wonder
if your dark eyes don't betray
your ancestors' dreams.
Do their memories
spill from your lips
and fall like these spring petals
into my hands?
I begin to see
our dug-out, our ritual fire,
the ochre, the drum, and the cornmeal.
You take the sweet bee pollen
of deep, sunken memory
and place it
on our tongues.

The Priest Who Thought He Was Alone

I saw him one night
in the Berkshire Mountains
at a place where the Shakers
would round up and dance.
At the edge of the crest,
I saw him,
as he stood with his
black robe flapping
like a great heron rising
like a universe brought near.

He seemed to emerge
from the pages of Ezekiel,
the great wheels turning,
the Upanishads spinning,
when he flung his
wind-borne voice
like a spray of wild birds,
birds that soared then settled,
like poured baptismal waters
returning to the river Jordan.

One Circle of Flesh

The scent of hemlock is a salve
as she reclines upon cloth strung
from tree limbs that rock her resting

spine and taut muscles given over to
sky, redbirds turn of wing, green dart
from trumpet vine to salvia, yields to

breathing no longer achingly distant
within planets of memory in undulating
mood. Fabric of earth is woven with

all those inhabited stories now
in her navel as the last breath
has been exhaled on blue

waves of thought weeping in the warp
of time unfurling fractals of narratives
deep with gazes, embraces

and the sea singing with Pleiades –
never a caesura, but everyone sifted
into salted selves.

They gave him the hemlock,
but before he sipped,
Phaedo pleaded with him to escape,

but he said what better fate
than to discuss virtue and justice
or to succumb to sleep with no dream.

She imagines the last day when all gather
in the square gently holding hands,
folding into pathos, how they will

miss *agon* and *eros* as the rose
dusk settles in one circle of flesh
and vanishes in coda.

Ancestor Walk

I stand on the windy crest of your mountains
Berry and Mahantango as your ancient breath
moves through the flags at these stones,
as the earth rises to greet you,
it rises to greet you through me,
your hills, your calcined barns, the ghosts
of your carriages, the torn pages of your character
sketches reside in these bones,
in the brittle, vermillion leaves of thought
that are swept in the glass of this water at midnight,
as I reach back the primitive path and see the faces
of your mothers' mothers' mothers, great and diminutive.
The mastodon stalks, you look away, the point of your arrow
cannot pierce the stance of this world, yet the crimson
still shines in the heart as you speak in the stirrings
of the place where you lived, the place that greets you
through me. The trees welcome your return,
their skeletal branches sift your scattered dust in four directions,
your four pollen pathways reach in all directions,
your ashes are blown as your refinements gather
at this cliff's edge where we stand together
gazing across receding horizons.

Augusts

The night stream is run with stars,
sky spills and slides
against sienna ground
with arrowheads deep in soil.
Cicadas buzz like unseen
molecules on August new moon.
Lanterns, not lights, glow behind
unshuttered windows, baby
possum crawls along black pond,
dog rests on moist pine needles
as unknowns peer from behind
fern and jewel weed.

This Sleep

I rest in the folded wing
of you where my skin begins
to lose its distinction
from yours.
It stays in the moist
in betweenness of us,
an admixture of salt
and breath, an almond
vapor that carries
currents of dream
cast with the night's moon,
a rush of repose
in the foam of another time
that seeps into now,
woven with sea grass
vining its way about us,
this nestling,
this breathing,
this sleep.

In the Center of the Fire

The girl tastes bee pollen
in a tiny palm of green
on her river island.

A sweet milk settles
in the belly of Manuelito
as the bleeding calf is bound.

An arrowhead is lodged
in whitewashed bone
where a daughter lie weeping.

She stacks five stones
in red mud
and sits as still.

Cirrus clouds and winter
stars mix with fire
and plumes of sorrow.

She awakens under
seventy swirls of
turquoise, pearl shell,
black blanket sky.

Longfellow Pine

Something happens to the blood in April,
a million cells scream to run the Indian paths
along the river, past corn and wheat fields,
over Blue Mountain and northward like a
wild horse ripping the hemp cord loose,
to get back to the oldest trees where history remains,
off the tarmac of Lincoln Highway, onto the old
running paths of the Pennsylvania Wilds, to rest
the head and nuzzle against the trunk of the
Longfellow Pine that reaches to a narrowing gaze
of blue at one hundred eighty feet, to hemlocks
that have stood here before William Penn,
before the Spaniards closed in on what became Florida,
standing now, no roads in, only foot path, deer path,
curling, no straight way, then lying belly down onto
the cool, sweet darkness, the ground of the dead
and the broken, the place of the risen, the blood
of the vanquished, the return of the lost ones,
to hear their stories in the stones, in the red dirt
melodies and the climbing vines of ghosts,
to again feel them dance, to hear their songs,
to remember.

It Is a Day like the Last Day

When I am earth enough to let each band of sun
enter each pore of me and return it in a kind of
generosity that cycles back, a lavender bergamot
élan vital releases dark bundles of world guilt,
black pockets of turbulence and holds these in a
columbine caress smoothing down callousness into
a sand wet with living mollusks and snails for burning
hearts and limbs to cool.

It is a day like the last day when I hold all of life
in a prayer of feet and salted eyes as ears take in
the cooing of the wind that spins with the bee
and rests with the lizard absorbed in the ancient heft
of igneous wall, all the same skin, all the skin
of thousands this side of the sea and that side of dark
space and this point which is no point in the sound
waves all enfolded, this day, the last day.

ACKNOWLEDGMENTS

Thanks to the editors of the following publications where these poems first appeared:

Atlanta Review: "What Is This *Therapeia*, This Attending To?" "Mathematics and the Girl"
Ellipsi: "Council"
Poem: "After Tsunami: A Salted World," "The Priest Who Thought He Was Alone," "To See Only at the Termination of Things," "Tribute to Freud's Dissenter"
Fledgling Rag: "A Distance from the Waters"
Mythopoetry Scholar: "Ancestor Walk," "In the Center of the Fire"

A special thanks to Composer Bruce Pennycook for setting the poem, "In the Center of the Fire," to music for choir. Thanks to the Butler School of Music at the University of Texas at Austin for the choral performance.

Deepest gratitude for my husband, Glen Mazis, my confidant and first reader. Within my writing always are my parents, John and Barbara Lenker Kennedy, who provided a still sanctuary for reading and reflection. Thanks to the graciousness of poets Harold Schweizer, Le Hinton, and Stephanie Pope in reading and commenting on this manuscript. Thanks to many friends over the years, especially from the Harrisburg Friends Meeting, who encouraged me. Thanks to Scott Hower and Ruth Meyers Kulp of the Canal House Poets who have read and commented on many of these poems and to Gary and Mary Smith, founders of the Theater of the Seventh Sister.

JUDITH A. KENNEDY lives in Lancaster County, Pennsylvania with her husband, philosopher and poet, Glen Mazis and their two dogs. She has studied philosophy, religion, and archetypal and clinical psychology at Slippery Rock, Syracuse, and Millersville Universities respectively. Her work is inspired by the history embedded in geography and by the geography of the imaginal. Judith works in Lancaster, Pennsylvania as a psychotherapist. She is grateful to the following forums where some of these poems had their beginnings: the Provincetown Fine Arts Workshop, the Theater of the Seventh Sister in Lancaster, PA, the Stadler Center for Poetry at Bucknell University and the Wildwood Writers Conference in Harrisburg, Pennsylvania. Her poetry has appeared in *The Atlanta Review, Ellipsis, Every Writer's Resource, Friends Journal, Mythopoetry Scholar,* and *Poem.* "In the Center of the Fire" was set to music for choir by Composer Bruce Pennycook of the Butler School of Music at the University of Texas at Austin. Judith also co-edited and wrote the biographical introduction to her great-grandfather's Civil War diary, *The Civil War Diary of Sgt. Christian Lenker, 19th Ohio Volunteer Infantry.* She has published a film review on the poetry of cinema in Terrence Mallick's film, *The Tree of Life*, with *Mythopoetry Scholar.* She and her colleague, Herb Landis, co-wrote, *Landscapes of Grief and Mourning: A Guide* for the film, *Death Valley: A Love Story.*

www.ingramcontent.com/pod-product-compliance
Lightning Source LLC
LaVergne TN
LVHW041508070426
835507LV00012B/1411